Science
on the
Edge

PROBING
VOLCANOES

LAURIE LINDOP

Twenty-First Century Books / Brookfield, Connecticut

Dedicated to Luke Abdow

Special thanks to Steven R. Brantley of the Hawaiian Volcano Observatory and David E. Wieprecht of the Cascades Volcano Observatory for their help with the photographs.

Back cover photograph courtesy of © Roger Ressmeyer/Corbis

Illustrations by Ron Miller

United States Department of the Interior, U.S. Geological Survey: pp. 4 (Dr. Margaret Mangan), 6 (Dr. Margaret Mangan), 28 (Chris G. Newhall), 31 (Ray Punongbayan); Gary L. Sego: p. 8; United States Department of the Interior, U.S. Geological Survey, David A. Johnston Cascades Volcano Observatory, Vancouver, Washington: pp. 33, 35, 38 (Chris G. Newhall), 40, 46 (bottom), 51 (David E. Wieprecht), 55 (D. A. Swanson), 58 (Austin Post/Glaciology Project), 60 (Lyn Topinka), 62-63 (Lyn Topinka); United States Department of the Interior, Hawaiian Volcano Observatory, Hawaiian Volcanoes National Park, Hawaii: pp. 15, 16 (D. A. Swanson), 48 (J. D. Griggs), 68; © Ph. Bourseiller: pp. 26-27; © Roger Ressmeyer/Corbis: pp. 19, 21, 22, 24, 46 (top); M. Sgt. Val Gempis, U. S. Air Force: p. 42; AP/Wide World Photos: pp. 44, 70; © Chris Johns/NGS Image Collection: p. 52; © Bill Ingalls/NASA: p. 64

Library of Congress Cataloging-in-Publication Data
Lindop, Laurie.
Probing volcanoes/by Laurie Lindop.
v. cm.—(Science on the edge)
Includes bibliographical references and index.
Contents: Predicting eruptions—Eruption! Volcanologists on the edge—History of volcano monitoring—Looking to the future—Becoming a volcanologist.
ISBN 0-7613-2700-2 (lib. bdg.)
1. Volcanoes—Juvenile literature.   2. Volcanologists—Juvenile literature.   [1. Volcanoes. 2. Volcanologists.]
I. Title.   II. Series.
QE521.3.L56   2003
551.21—dc21   2002014251

Published by Twenty-First Century Books
A Division of The Millbrook Press, Inc.
2 Old New Milford Road
Brookfield, Connecticut 06804
www.millbrookpress.com

CONTENTS

The Soufrière Hills volcano of Montserrat releases ash into the air while volcanologists set up an observation post to monitor the volcano's activity.

Introduction

In 1995 a volcano on the Caribbean island of Montserrat stirred awake. Ash plumes and steam rose into the bright blue sky. Earthquakes shook the land and rattled windows. Local officials put in a call for help.

Right away a team of American volcanologists jumped into action. They loaded state-of-the-art scientific equipment into a cargo jet and flew to Montserrat. As the jet circled the island, they saw lovely sand beaches and emerald water. Looming over this lush paradise was the steaming volcano.

Scientists from the United States Geological Survey collect ash from an "ash trap" they placed beside the volcano. Ash traps are emptied after each volcanic emission so scientists can determine the thickness of the ash deposited by each explosion.

As soon as the plane landed, the volcanologists installed various devices around the volcano to take its pulse. Their goal was to determine whether or not it was headed toward a big eruption, and if it was, to make sure that people remained a safe distance away.

On June 25, 1997, a blast shook the island and a massive ash cloud rose into the sky. It blocked out the sunshine and the island was plunged into darkness deeper than any night. Blobs of molten rock sprayed into the air. They disintegrated and fell back down toward Earth in thousands of glowing chunks. Clouds of burning gas and ash rolled down the volcano's slopes, filling valleys and flattening houses before finally plunging into the boiling ocean. Fiery rocks rained down on the town of Plymouth, setting it ablaze.

Fortunately the volcanologists had seen the warning signs ahead of time and evacuated the town and surrounding areas. Only nineteen people died from the volcano, and they were people who ventured beyond the roadblocks set up by police.

One villager describes what life is like in the days after the eruption as the volcano continued to sputter:

The Soufrière Hills volcano, by now a familiar if unpredictable neighbor, sends cascades of dark ash into the air and a shower of pebbles onto the house I am camped out in. I listen in awe as the sounds grow louder, the volcanic rock fall peppering the roof and walls and windows of the house like a hard rain. I peek through the wooden louvers of the door that opens onto a swimming pool, gray with ash. Chunks of [volcanic rock] float like toy boats in the water, sending ripples crisscrossing the length of the pool. Watching the fallout, I can only think how fortunate I am to see another day.[1]

An ash cloud blackened the skies over the nearby town of Plymouth in the days after the Soufrière Hills volcano erupted.

Volcanologists understand that their hard work can save people's lives. "There is nothing we can do to stop a volcano, but we try to get people and property out of the way as fast as we can," said Margaret Mangan, one of the volcanologists who was in Montserrat.[2]

A Grand and Destructive Spectacle

On average, fifty volcanoes erupt each year. Scientists estimate that at least 200,000 people have lost their lives as a result of volcanic eruptions in the last 500 years. Since 1980 volcanic activity has forced more than one million people to flee their homes.

The United States is home to more volcanoes than any other country except Indonesia and Japan. The majority of these volcanoes are in Alaska. Until recently, there was no way to predict when a volcano would blow. Within the last twenty years, however, volcanologists have been working hard to learn how to predict eruptions and keep people safe.

In the following chapters you will join volcanologists as they head out into the field to monitor these geological time bombs. "Like any grand and destructive spectacle, volcanoes have alternately attracted and terrified humanity through the ages," said volcanologist Stanley Williams. "The difference between ordinary people and volcanologists is that, with us, the appeal far outweighs the terror. . . . Most people flee from erupting volcanoes. We head straight for them."[3]

What's Inside a Volcano?

The word *volcano* comes from the little island of Vulcano in the Mediterranean Sea. This island had a mountain that erupted regularly. The early Romans believed this mountain belonged to Vulcan, the blacksmith to the gods. Watching steam and sparks shoot from the mountain's crater, the Romans assumed that Vulcan must be hard at work inside, beating out thunderbolts for Jupiter, king of the gods, or weapons for Mars, the god of war. Today scientists know that a volcano's power comes from its connection to the inner Earth.

The Earth is made up of different layers, kind of like a peanut M&M. Deep at the center there's a dense core that we can envision as the peanut. Surrounding the core is a hot semi-molten layer called the mantle, like the chocolate. The Earth's thin rocky crust is similar to the candy coating. The Earth's crust is actually like a slightly cracked M&M because it's broken up into big chunks called tectonic plates. These plates float on the Earth's hotter, softer mantle, moving a few inches every year. When the plates move, sometimes they grind together, sometimes they slip apart, and other times they'll slide over and sink under each other.[4]

Most above-sea active volcanoes occur at places where one big plate descends beneath another plate. When the sinking, or subducting, plate reaches about 60 miles (97 kilometers) into the Earth's hot mantle, it causes the overlying plate to melt. This molten rock is

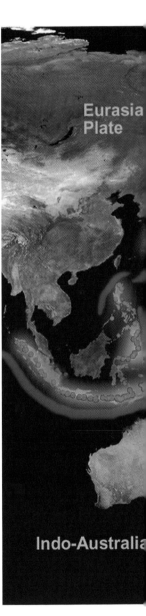

Eurasia Plate

Indo-Australia

This map shows the boundaries of Earth's tectonic plates in purple. Most of the active volcanoes, shown here as red dots, lie where the plates meet. The Ring of Fire is a belt of volcanoes that encircles the Pacific plate.

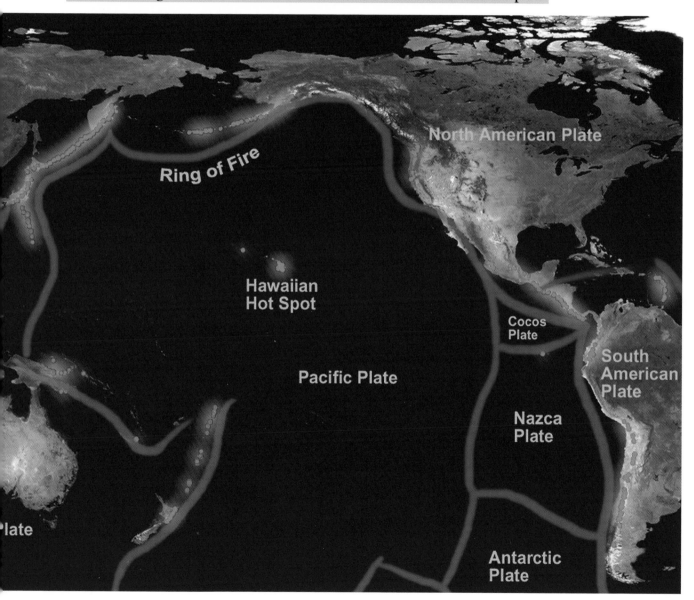

called magma. Magma is buoyant, which means it wants to rise. Globs of gas-filled magma make their way through cracks and channels up toward the Earth's surface. Some of these globs harden en route and turn into rock. Other globs find channels that lead to reservoirs called magma chambers that are beneath volcanoes. Volcanoes are vents in the Earth's surface. They are usually plugged with cooled magma that has turned into solid rock.

Under Pressure and Ready to Blow

Volcanoes erupt when the pressure inside them becomes so great that the magma surges up and forces its way out. What causes the pressure to increase in a volcano? In some cases, volcanoes, like those in Hawaii, have magma chambers that can hold only a certain amount of magma. As new gas-rich magma arrives from deep inside the Earth, the magma chamber expands and the pressure rises. If too much magma makes its way into the chamber, the pressure will cause the sides of the magma chamber to break and the magma escapes (rather like an overinflated balloon). Once magma reaches the Earth's surface, it's called lava.

In other volcanoes the magma chambers don't get filled very often because there isn't a steady supply of magma to them. While the magma sits in the chamber, some of its gases will start to bubble off. These gas bubbles slowly but surely increase the pressure inside the volcano. The pressure may eventually reach a sufficient level to trigger an eruption. Other times the gas pressure alone isn't quite enough and the volcano needs another incentive to blow, such as the sudden arrival of more magma from deep inside the Earth. The increase in heat from even a small amount of new magma can be enough to cause an eruption.

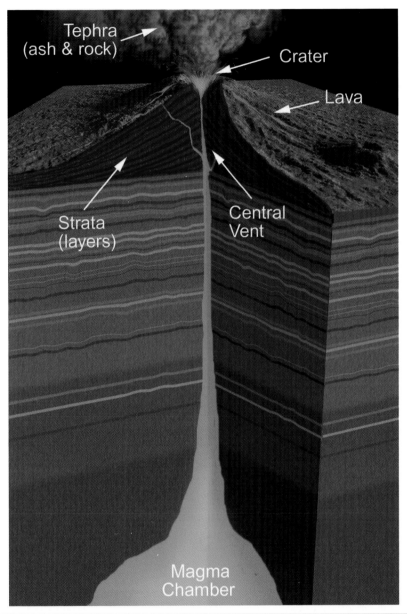

Tephra (ash & rock)

Crater

Lava

Strata (layers)

Central Vent

Magma Chamber

This is the profile of a stratovolcano, which builds up in layers (strata) of erupted cinders and ash. Magma travels up the central vent from the magma chamber, which is beneath the Earth's surface. The magma erupts at the crater and breaks apart into tephra—pieces of rock and ash that blast into the air.

From Gentle Flows to Violent Eruptions

"I have been lucky enough to witness eruptions from [a number] of different volcanoes," said one volcanologist. "Eruptions at Kilauea volcano in Hawaii included quiet flows of lava and sometimes wonderful shooting of gas rich lava into fire-fountains. I saw similar activity at Erta Ale (Ethiopia) where a constantly active lava lake swirled within a crater. At Etna and Stromboli volcanoes (both in Italy) the small . . . eruptions against the evening sky were spell-binding. All eruptions are exciting because we normally don't see rock hot enough to flow like liquid or shoot into the air like endless fireworks."[5]

Some volcanic eruptions are explosive and others are not. It depends on how thick the lava is. Runny lava allows gases to escape during an eruption and tends to pour out in picturesque rivers. Other volcanoes have thick, pasty lava with a lot of gases in it. The gases want to escape, but the lava is too sticky. The gas bubbles expand and finally burst. Their pent-up power unleashes explosive eruptions where lava, rock, ash, and gas blast outward. These eruptions can be deadly.

Lava is always red-hot when it spurts out of a volcano, but as it cools, it quickly changes to dark red, gray, black, or another color. One volcanologist recalled witnessing a nonexplosive lava flow with a group of his students. "We tossed banana peels into the flow and watched them turn to ash with a hiss. Rocks tumbled out of the black stream, revealing the incandescent orange-yellow core of the lava tongue. We clocked the flow's speed, about 15 feet [4.6 meters] per hour, and took its temperature, 1,970°F [1,077°C]. You could only insert the temperature probe when the wind was blowing away from your body; otherwise you started to cook."[6]

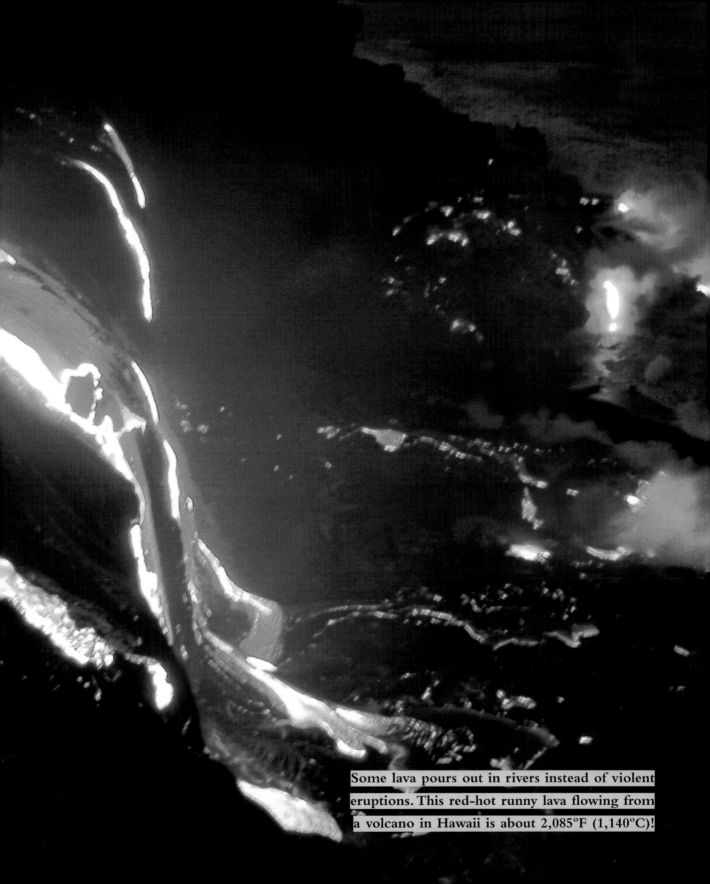

Some lava pours out in rivers instead of violent eruptions. This red-hot runny lava flowing from a volcano in Hawaii is about 2,085°F (1,140°C)!

Understanding a volcano's past eruptive patterns is essential to determining its future activity. These volcanologists are examining the tephra layers that erupted more than seven hundred years ago from Kilauea volcano in Hawaii.

CHAPTER ONE

Predicting Eruptions

When volcanologists arrive at a threatening volcano, they've got to work against the clock to figure out if it will erupt and when that eruption is likely to occur. "It's really challenging to predict what nature is going to do," admitted volcanologist Chris Newhall.[1]

The first step is to figure out how that volcano behaved in the past. Chances are, a future eruption will be similar in scope. Volcanologists look for clues about past eruptions in the geology of the area surrounding the volcano. They drill for rock samples, test ash residue, and study the lay of the land. In this way they can figure out the size of previous eruptions and when they occurred.

Compiling all this information, the volcanologists draw up "hazard maps." These maps predict the types of destruction likely to be inflicted on areas around the volcano, including the zones of greatest risk. The volcanologists give these hazard maps to local officials so they can plan how to evacuate people living within the danger zones.

Probing an Active Volcano

Besides studying a volcano's past eruptive history, scientists go out into the field and use sophisticated instruments to determine what's happening inside a volcano at that moment. The science of volcano monitoring evolves all the time, but there are some basic elements volcanologists look at when they want to take a volcano's pulse:

1. Earthquakes: Earthquakes commonly provide the earliest warning of volcanic unrest. When magma gets very close to the Earth's surface, it puts pressure on the surrounding cooler rocks, causing some of them to crack. As these cracks open up, the Earth shakes.

    Seismometers are devices that determine the size and location of quakes. Volcanologists put at least three (and often eight to ten) seismometers around a volcano to track the subsurface movement of magma. Certain quake patterns exist only before eruptions. When volcanologists see these patterns, they know an eruption is likely to occur.

Volcanologists from the Hawaii Volcano Observatory study a fresh crust of lava that is still warm enough in some places to melt their shoes.

2. Gases: When magma is deep underground, it is under pressure and the gases remain dissolved in its liquid. As the magma rises toward the surface, gases such as carbon dioxide (CO_2) and sulfur dioxide (SO_2) begin to bubble off. Volcanologists use devices like the correlation spectrometer (COSPEC) to watch for a spike in the concentration of gases that often occurs before an eruption.

3. Heat: Before an eruption, a volcano often starts to release more heat as the magma rises inside it. This magma can heat the local groundwater above the boiling point and create steam. Volcanologists look for changes in the amount of heat and steam a volcano produces as indicators of unrest. Recently volcanologists have been using weather satellites to take infrared pictures of the amount of heat volcanoes give off. This method is particularly useful for keeping tabs on volcanoes in remote areas. If the satellite detects a sudden increase in heat from a volcano, volcanologists know they should start paying attention to it.

4. Ground deformation: When magma rises inside a volcano, it may push out sections of rock. Occasionally the deformed section visibly bulges out. More often it is only a small inflation. Volcanologists use a variety of sensitive instruments to detect even minute changes in a volcano's shape.

While the monitoring instruments volcanologists use are high tech, putting them in place around a volcano requires old-fashioned sweat. Volcanologists may have to use machetes to bushwhack a trail up the slopes. To walk across a glacial snowcap at the peak, they use ice picks and strap crampons (metal spikes) onto their boots. Often volcanologists rely on helicopters to ferry them to otherwise inaccessible points. Some volcanoes are so tall that scientists must be careful to avoid altitude sickness.

Scientist Hugo Delgado Grenados works on the world's tallest volcano, Mexico's Pico de Orizaba. He has become accustomed to the lack of oxygen when he's taking heat measurements

Volcanologist Stan Williams collects gas samples from a fumarole—a vent in a volcano where hot gases escape.

at the crater, 18,410 feet (5,611 meters) above sea level. However, his assistants have suffered from blood in their lungs, a condition called edema, a common side effect of trying to work in a region that mountaineers refer to as the "death zone."

Up at the Crater

In movies volcanoes are often depicted as cauldrons filled with bubbling molten rock. In real life most volcanic craters are dry and quiet misshapen rock pits. The crater is where the volcano's

Volcanologists Chris Newhall and Arturo Daag collect soil samples from within Mount Pinatubo.

vent(s) have gotten clogged after past eruptions. In some craters the rock may be split with streams of glowing molten rock or there may be small churning lava lakes.

One volcanologist recalled his trek into a crater in the Andes:

The crater seemed a sterile place, its colors running a dreary spectrum from dark gray to brown to beige. But . . . closer inspection . . . revealed pockets of color—rust hewed swaths of rock breaking down in the heat and gases of the crater, and canary yellow patches of sulfur that had accumulated next to a gas vent, known as a fumarole. The vents were small fissures where high-pressure gases were released from the magma body beneath the volcano. The gases, which assaulted the nostrils with a [mixture] of sharp acrid odors right out of the chemistry lab, shot from the fumaroles with a hiss, obscuring the landscape in a swirl of vapors. . . . When you step down into such a crater, the howl of the wind at 14,000 or 16,000 feet is replaced by the eerie quiet of the Earth's interior. The exception is when volcanoes are riven by high-pressure, high-temperature fumaroles. Then you feel as if you are planted behind a jet engine as it prepares for take-off.[2]

Exploring an active crater is always dangerous. According to volcanologist Chuck Wood, "The pattern of events that signifies an eruption at one volcano may not occur before an eruption at a different volcano. And the same volcano may change its eruptive behavior at any time!"[3] This unpredictability can have deadly consequences, as a group of researchers in Colombia, South America, discovered.

A Ticking Time Bomb

In January 1993 a prominent volcanologist, Stanley Williams, prepared to lead a crew of multinational researchers up Colombia's Galeras volcano. He felt pretty confident they'd be safe. For a decade he and his colleagues had been carefully monitoring Galeras.

Several weeks before the expedition, the COSPEC devices detected a rise in the telltale SO_2 gases escaping from vents along

Volcanologist Christina Heliker shields herself from the intense heat as she collects a batch of hot lava to examine during an eruption of the Kilauea volcano.

its flanks. The seismometers indicated that tremors were growing more intense as magma rose inside it. But then Galeras had quieted. No more gas was escaping and the tremors were way down. Williams assumed the volcano was napping.

Unfortunately, as Williams later said, Galeras was "tricking us spectacularly."[4] He now suspects that the volcano had pushed up almost as much magma as it could hold. This sealed the vents. Bottled up, the magma couldn't move so the tremors stopped. The gas levels died off. Inside, the volcano was behaving like a pressure cooker. The pent-up gases caused the pressure to sky-rocket to dangerous levels.

Williams and his team strapped on backpacks of equipment and climbed to the crater. "We were sitting on a bomb that was [silently] ticking away," he recalled.[5] All morning the scientists milled about taking measurements.

By midday half of the group began their descent. Williams waited at the crater's rim for the rest of the team to finish. He watched a highly regarded Russian volcanologist thrust his test tube into a fumarole. Gases as hot as 440°F (227°C) filled the tube and bubbled into a solution the volcanologist had prepared. Suddenly boulders started tumbling around the crater and the ground shook. Williams shouted for everyone to get out, and he ran down the gravel slope.

"I had made it only a few yards when the air was rent by a sound like a thunderclap or a sonic boom. Immediately afterward I heard a deafening *craaack,* the sound of the Earth's crust snapping. Instinctively, I hunched my shoulders and hiked my backpack over my neck and head. I did not get far."[6] Red-hot boulders the size of televisions blew out of the crater and fiery

Two volcanologists in red stand at the rim of a crater and observe the activity within. Molten lava inside the crater is breaking through the black crust.

gases roared along the rim. Blobs of molten rock spurted into the sky and, as they cooled, rained down in baseball-size chunks on top of the researchers. Steaming boulders crushed Williams's leg, fractured his skull, and burned much of his body. He was the lucky one.

"The ground began to shake," he recalled, "and ten seconds later, everybody was dead. That's how little warning we had."[7] In tremendous pain and unable to use his legs, Williams slithered down the mountain slope. He hid behind a big rock until the fiery gas-filled explosion died down and he could be rescued.

After sixteen operations and still recovering from his injuries, Williams has translated the events at Galeras into a model that he believes will help predict eruptions at other similar volcanoes. He wants to make sure that no other volcanologists are deceived by volcanoes that seem to be asleep but are actually turning into dangerous pressure cookers on the verge of explosion.

One day volcanologists may identify every pre-eruptive pattern possible. To date, however, there is not a single checklist of warning signs that will guarantee a volcano is about to blow. The way volcanoes behave is very individualized. "There's no magic bullet in predicting volcanic eruptions," said volcanologist Charles Connor. "The key thing is to cross-correlate [compare] as many different observations as possible."[8]

This fissure opened up on Mount Pinatubo in 1990.
In the background active vents pour out steam.

CHAPTER TWO

Eruption! Volcanologists on the Edge

Two weeks after the Philippines was hit by a big earthquake in 1990, a group of nuns there reported a strange new sight on the local mountain: a line of craters had appeared along the slopes. Even stranger, a massive steam explosion had opened up a fissure on Mount Pinatubo that was a half-mile long. This fissure looked infernal—clouds of foul-smelling steam poured out of it, burning the surrounding vegetation.

After listening to the nuns' account, a Filipino volcanologist named Ray Punongbayan began monitoring Mount Pinatubo more closely. He wasn't too worried about this long-sleeping volcano. He figured that the quake might have affected Pinatubo's inner plumbing. Some underground water might have been exposed to Pinatubo's heat, creating the steam. It seemed far more likely that Mount Pinatubo was reacting to the big earthquake than stirring toward an eruption.

In April 1991, Punongbayan contacted the U.S. Volcano Disaster Assistance Program (VDAP). He told their leaders that he didn't have enough equipment or manpower to figure out what was happening inside the volcano, but now regular quakes were occurring along the slopes. He needed help.

Shake and Bake

Three weeks later, VDAP sent a team of volcanologists to the Philippines along with thirty-five trunks of scientific equipment. The volcanologists set up a lab in an apartment on a military base where they had a good view of Mount Pinatubo. They hooked up phones, radio receivers, faxes, and computers. They filled bookcases with scientific volumes on volcanology. They hung a map of Pinatubo on the wall.

One of the VDAP volcanologists was Andy Lockhart. Andy was a fun-loving guy who was also a genius at getting the sometimes testy seismometers to run well. He didn't mind hiking up a volcano to plant the devices, but as soon as he took one look at Mount Pinatubo, he realized he'd need a helicopter. The volcano's slopes were sliced by deep river canyons. The ridges in between were covered in lush green jungle growth that looked impenetrable. There was only one road winding up Mount Pinatubo, and

Ray Punongbayan with most of the early members of the observation gang at Pinatubo. Members, from left to right, are Dave Harlow, Chris Newhall, Ray Punongbayan, John Ewert, Andy Lockhart, John Power, Gemme Ambubuyog, and Joey Marcial.

it was along the volcano's west side, away from where steam vents sent white clouds billowing up into the sky.

Fortunately the U.S. Air Force had a long-established military base at the foot of Mount Pinatubo. When Andy Lockhart went to Clark Air Force Base to inquire about using a helicopter, the pilots eyed the scruffy volcanologist in flip-flop sandals and told him that the helicopters were all being used and that he should come back tomorrow. Every day Lockhart got up and trekked over to the base. Every day he was told to try another time. Frustrated, Lockhart would go back to the lab and unroll a map of Pinatubo. He'd hunch over it and plot where he hoped to one day put the seismometers.

Eventually the pilots came to admire Lockhart's commitment. They agreed to give him and a couple of his assistants a ride in their helicopter. Getting into the air turned out to be just the first challenge. As the pilot hovered over a steep ridge, Lockhart looked down and realized that the spot where he wanted to put one of his seismometers was covered in tall, waving grass. If he dropped down there, he'd be like a small mouse in an overgrown wheat field. How would he plant his seismometers surrounded by such high grass?

Lockhart came up with a plan. He asked the pilot to lower the copter so that the air from the whirring propellers would flatten down the high grass. Lockhart and his assistants jumped out with the seismometer. The volcanologists tackled the grass using shovels. When they'd finally cleared a small patch, they dug a hole. Lockhart lowered the seismometer into the earth and affixed transmitters, which would allow it to send radio signals back to the lab twenty-four hours a day.

Andy Lockhart tries to get the seismometers in place around Mount Pinatubo.

It Doesn't Look Good!

Relying on the relationship Andy had built up with the Air Force, colleague Chris Newhall convinced a pilot to take him up to study the gas shooting from Pinatubo's flanks. Newhall strapped the 60-pound (27-kilogram) COSPEC device to the belly of a helicopter and directed the pilot to fly through the volcano's steam. The COSPEC needle swung up and then down as they passed through the hazy cloud.

When he got back to the lab, Newhall did some calculations and found that Pinatubo was releasing large amounts of SO_2. On subsequent tests, the gas levels continued to increase. This proved that the steam was not caused by an earthquake, but rather by magma rising inside the volcano and releasing gas. The volcanologists realized they were facing a very dangerous situation.

Their studies of the volcano's past showed that Mount Pinatubo was capable of spewing massive pyroclastic flows. A pyroclastic flow is a high-speed avalanche of hot ash, rock fragments, and gas that moves down the sides of a volcano during an eruption. Pyroclastic flows can be as hot as 1,500°F (816°C) and move at speeds of 100 to 450 miles (161 to 724 kilometers) per hour! They knock over and burn everything in their path. They'll mow down whole forests of massive old trees like blades of grass. Volcanologists say that if you were to be caught by a pyroclastic flow, you'd probably feel a hot wind right before you were incinerated.

Newhall had drawn up hazard maps that showed where pyroclastic flows had reached in previous eruptions. The Aeta people lived in the middle of the remains of past pyroclastic flows. For hundreds of years the Aeta people had been farming the volcano's slopes. They had their own language and lived much as their ancestors had done in small huts. Newhall realized that if this impending eruption turned out to be a big one like some of those in Pinatubo's past, not only would the Aeta's villages be destroyed, but Clark Air Force Base would also be reduced to nothing but rubble.

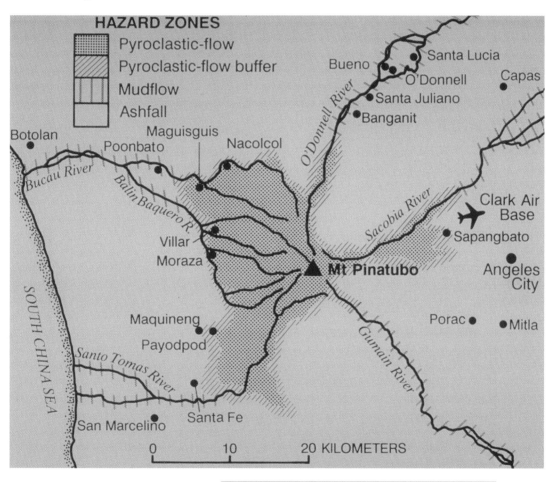

A map created by the volcanologists of the potential hazard zones around Mount Pinatubo

Armed with his hazard maps, Newhall invited the Air Force's top commanders to a barbecue where he gave them the chilling news. Later, one of the colonels wrote in his journal: "I had no idea how to deal with this information on either a personal or a professional level. What they had just said scared me, really scared me. Not so much for myself or any immediate danger. But how would we manage this thing?"[1]

Evacuation

The volcanologists knew there was no way to "manage" a volcano. The only thing they could do was try to keep people a safe distance away. As seismic activity increased around Pinatubo and a bulge appeared on its flank, the volcanologists recommended that all people living in Newhall's hazard zones be evacuated. More than 50,000 villagers from around Mount Pinatubo, including members of the Aeta tribe, fled to towns at a safer distance. Twenty thousand American service people from Clark Air Force Base were also evacuated to a military base on the other side of the island.

If you had visited Clark after the evacuation, you would have found it as deserted as a ghost town. The shops were closed, and the parade ground, which was usually filled with soldiers marching in regiment, was eerily silent. Just about the only people staying behind were the VDAP volcanologists and some military police to guard against looters.

The volcanologists had moved their lab to a backup facility that was as far away from Pinatubo as they could get while still being on the air force base. From this new lab, they had a view straight down the air force base's empty runway and up to the threatening volcano. They would have preferred to monitor Pinatubo from somewhere even farther away, but their choices were restricted. They wanted to take seismic readings and gather data as the volcano erupted—a rare scientific opportunity. In order to do so, they needed electricity to power their computers. The air base had a powerful electrical generator while the electricity on the rest of the island was unreliable, even in the best of times.

"Under different or better circumstances, we should have been further away from the volcano," recalled Ed Wolfe, one of the volcanologists. "But there wasn't a good alternative available to us. . . . So we were closer to the volcano . . . than we wished. I don't think anybody was confident a pyroclastic flow couldn't reach us."[2] Indeed the new lab fell within the hazard zone if Pinatubo's eruption turned out to be a massive one.

Having evacuated the air force base and all the local people, the volcanologists were as ready as they'd ever be. They stared out the windows at Pinatubo, waiting. Instead of ratcheting up its activity, the volcano showed signs of quieting down.

Volcanologists say that volcanoes "toy" with them when they appear to be on the verge of erupting and then slack off. Sometimes volcanoes toy for only a day or two, but occasionally they toy for months or even years—revving up and then calming down and then revving up again. In fact, some toying volcanoes don't erupt at all.

"This was a stressful time . . . ," one of the volcanologists remembered. "We were concerned about the volcano and the safety of those around it, including ourselves. We were also con-cerned about the serious consequences of a false alarm and

A vapor plume from active steam vents on Mount Pinatubo

whether we would have a second chance should the volcano not erupt as anticipated. Sleep was difficult, nerves were taut, and we were at our physical and emotional limits."[3]

The bad food was also getting everyone down. With all the local restaurants closed, the volcanologists had raided the air force base's pantry. They took a huge supply of cheese balls back to their office, which they devoured with nervous energy. In addition to cheese balls, they survived on military MREs or meals-ready-to-eat. These are freeze-dried high-calorie meals, like the ones astronauts take into outer space.

During the difficult days while Pinatubo toyed with them, seismographer Andy Lockhart decided to play a joke on his colleague Dave Harlow. He found a big dead spider and put it in Dave's container of cheese balls. Dave opened the lid, stared inside, and put the lid back on. Lockhart was stunned, but he also realized, "Dave's got bigger problems."[4]

One big problem was the complaints the volcanologists had been hearing from Clark Air Force Base's commanders. The evacuees were miserable at the makeshift shelter on the other base. There wasn't enough room, so military personnel were sleeping in hallways, offices, and classrooms. The message was clear: You scientists had better be right about this volcano blowing soon, because otherwise you're going to have to answer to a lot of angry people.

Eruption!

On June 12, a little over two months since VDAP scientists first arrived in the Philippines, Pinatubo let loose with the first of what would be a series of eruptions. In absolute silence, a gray ash cloud blasted 50,000 feet (15,240 meters) straight up into the air. When it reached 12 miles (19 kilometers) above the Earth, it slammed into a level of cold air in the upper atmosphere and began rolling sideways. The volcanologists were thrilled that the toying period was over. For the next two days the volcano continued to expel small pyroclastic flows. The volcanologists guessed that Pinatubo was still warming up and soon would have bigger fireworks in store for them.

The initial excitement quickly wore off when it became clear that some of the seismometers weren't working correctly.

A huge ash cloud from the first eruption of Mount Pinatubo was visible from Clark Air Force Base.

It was a nightmare. The volcano was heading toward a massive eruption at any moment and the VDAP team couldn't pinpoint the exact location of these quakes. "And they [the quakes] were big," Harlow recalled. "It would have given us tremendous insight on how these systems evolve after the first . . . blast and all those individual [small pyroclastic] eruptions leading to the major eruption. Finally there was a break in the activity and I said, 'Man, let's get out there and fix this.' There was a fair amount of resistance to doing this because of the obvious dangers, because the thing could really erupt."[5]

In order to fix the seismometers, they'd have to take an air force helicopter up to the volcano. If Pinatubo blew, they'd have virtually no chance of survival. To make matters worse, a storm was bearing down on the island. Harlow was determined to make the trip, however.

The helicopter lifted off into the buffeting wind. Right away, visibility dropped as thunderheads mixed with ash spewing from the volcano. Lightning zigzagged all around the helicopter. The pilot managed to swoop up the volcano's slopes and land near one of the malfunctioning devices. Harlow jumped out and tried desperately to get it working. Back at the lab, Andy Lockhart radioed that it still wasn't functioning. Eventually Harlow gave up and climbed back into the helicopter.

By the time Harlow returned, a driving rain slashed down over the deserted air force base. Hurricane-force winds bent the trees and tore street signs loose from their poles. A typhoon was coming. The volcanologists stared up at the ash-spewing volcano and realized that lahars were now a serious threat.

On June 14, volcanologists employed the help of the U.S. Air Force to helicopter them up to the volcano and make emergency repairs to the seismometers.

Lahars, or mudflows, form when volcanic ash combines with water, such as intense rainfall. Lahars rush downstream at speeds of 20 to 40 miles (32 to 64 kilometers) per hour, much faster than anyone can run. Lahars tear up rocks, soil, and vegetation from the river channels. They can wrench houses and buildings from their foundations. Some lahars are filled with so much debris they look like racing torrents of wet cement. When Colombia's Nevado del Ruiz volcano erupted in 1985, its ice cap was rapidly melted. This flood of melted snow unleashed lahars that were, in places, 130 feet (40 meters) high. That lahar ended up drowning 23,000 people in thick mud.

The volcanologists at Mount Pinatubo prayed that the hazard maps they'd drawn of the potential paths of lahars were accurate and that everyone who lived in the danger zone had been evacuated.

On the morning of June 15, with the typhoon storm bearing down upon the Philippines, Mount Pinatubo began its main eruption sequence. The few working seismographs recorded a series of powerful earthquakes. At 5:55 A.M. the volcano sent up a fountain-shaped gray cloud 115,000 feet (35,052 meters) into the air. The volcanologists watched as the cloud collapsed back down around the volcano's slopes and filled the storm-lashed sky with burning clouds of thick ash. The ash rolled down Pinatubo's slopes and descended on the empty air force base. Streetlights automatically flipped on, but then seemed to disappear in the black ash cloud as if someone had turned them off again. One military commander later recalled, "It was so dark, I thought I'd died and gone to hell."[6]

Thick wet ash covered everything. It mixed with the rain and hammered against the lab windows. The volcanologists wondered how much power Pinatubo had in store. Their own hazard maps showed that at its worst, Pinatubo could send pyroclastic flows straight into their lab. Once such a flow started, it would take four short minutes to reach them. Their only hope was that the eruption wouldn't be quite that powerful, that their lab was just out of reach.

At 1:42 P.M., Mount Pinatubo exploded in the largest volcanic eruption on Earth in more than three quarters of a century. The highly pressurized magma inside Pinatubo started shooting

Filipinos who lived in villages near the erupting volcano covered their faces from the ash and fled the area on buffalo.

out of the crater like soda from a shaken can. Anxiously checking his computers, Andy Lockhart realized that seismometers on the slopes were dying one after the other as they were overcome with pyroclastic flows. This was the moment of truth: In another four minutes the volcanologists would either be safe or pyroclastic flows would roar along the air force base's runway, headed straight into their office. There was no point in trying to run.

Gathering at the lab's window, they stared out at the ash-filled darkness and the line of twinkling red lights running along the base landing strip. If those lights disappeared, there'd be nothing they could do. They'd feel the hot pyroclastic wind and it would all be over.

After a few minutes the scientists heaved sighs of relief. The lights were still twinkling—the flows hadn't reached them. Later they'd discover that the pyroclastic flows had stopped just on the other side of the base. There was no guarantee, however, that the volcano wouldn't let loose with an even bigger pyroclastic surge. So they left.

Leaving proved dangerous as well. The typhoon sent ashy mud hurtling through the darkness. The weight of wet ash caved in the roofs of air force hangars and wrecked buildings. The volcanologists could hear the trainlike roar of lahars crashing through the mountain canyons and overflowing the riverbeds. Earthquakes shook the ground and collapsed houses.

It took three hours for the volcanologists to get a safe distance away. Stopping at a college, the exhausted scientists went into an empty classroom and rolled up in sleeping bags to fall asleep to the constant shaking of earthquakes.

Lahars covered huge areas of land surrounding the volcano.

Many homes were buried by lahars and vegetation was destroyed.

The Aftermath

One million people were threatened by the volcano that afternoon, but because of the scientists' hard work, only 350 people lost their lives, most of them from collapsed buildings. The explosion blew 1,000 feet (305 meters) off the volcano's 5,725-foot (1,745-meter) peak and ash blanketed thousands of square miles. In some places the ash was 600 feet (183 meters) thick! It clogged streambeds, buried homes, and turned everything gray. A small group of U.S. airmen stayed behind to dig out Clark Air Force Base from under the ash. But soon the military packed up and left the Philippines, bringing to a close a nearly one hundred-year-long era of being there.

The homes of the Aeta people were ruined. "The Aeta culture has been destroyed because we have lost our land," said one tribe member. "Our ancestors told us not to leave our land because it is ours. The tombs of my father, mother, grandparents, and other ancestors are now buried under lahar."[7] More than a decade after the eruption, most members of the tribe have moved to resettlement sites and adapted to the modern culture.

The damage to the Pinatubo area did not end with the eruption. Each rainy season since 1991 has resulted in lahars from the ash deposited by the eruption. The economy has been ruined and will not return to normal for decades.

Lava runs from a fountain that burst through Earth's surface at Kilauea volcano in Hawaii.

CHAPTER THREE

History of Volcano Monitoring

In A.D. 79, Mount Vesuvius erupted in central Italy. In minutes, pyroclastic flows overwhelmed the town of Pompeii, killing 3,360 people. Others died from breathing in the toxic volcanic gas, and many choked to death as their throats filled with ash.

One man, who was nineteen at the time, recalled escaping with his mother:

Ashes were already falling, not as yet very thickly, I look round; a dense black cloud was coming up behind us, spreading over the Earth like a flood. . . . Darkness fell, not the dark of a moonless or cloudy night, but as if the lamp had been put out in a closed room. You could hear the shrieks of women, the wailing of infants, and the shouting of men. . . . People bewailed their own fate or that of their relatives, and there were some who prayed for death in their terror of dying. Many besought the aid of the gods, but still more imagined there were no gods left, and that the universe was plunged into eternal darkness forever more. . . . It grew lighter, though that seemed not a return of day, but a sign that the fire was approaching.[1]

Most consider the author of this account, Pliny the Younger, to be the first volcanologist. He gave a precise description of the phenomena before, during, and after an eruption.

Between Pliny's ancient world and modern times, there haven't been many volcanologists. Volcanoes are so unpredictable and erupt so rarely that most scientists had to be content with studying the effects of eruptions long after they occurred. Every once in a while a scientist lucked out and happened to be in the right place at the right time. For example, when Mount Pelée, in the West Indies, erupted in 1902, a former assistant to Thomas Edison, Frank Perret, happened to be living there. He'd noticed tremors in the days leading up to the eruption and had monitored these earthquakes by biting down on his metal bedpost. He discovered that he could feel otherwise unnoticeable vibrations with his teeth!

In Hawaii, lava from an eruption of Kilauea volcano buries Chain of Craters Road once again. It was closed once before in 1969 from an eruption of Mauna Ulu volcano.

Hawaii's Realms of Wonder

In 1912 geologist Thomas Jaggar of the Massachusetts Institute of Technology (M.I.T.) decided that the only way to learn about volcanoes was to study one that erupted regularly. He established a lab at one of the world's most active volcanoes, Kilauea, on Hawaii's Big Island. Because he had limited funds, Jaggar used prisoners to prepare the foundation for the original Hawaiian Volcano Observatory (HVO) on Kilauea's crater.

In the blazing Hawaiian heat, the prisoners dug through almost 6 feet (1.8 meters) of volcanic ash and pumice until they reached a layer of firm lava where Jaggar could place seismometers that he'd purchased from Japan. These seismometers would look quite primitive to us now (they were basically pendulums designed to detect horizontal motions of the Earth), but at the time they were some of the most high-tech devices available.

The Hawaiian volcanoes are "hot spot" volcanoes, which means they form when a plume of magma burns through the Earth's crust like a blowtorch. The eruptions don't tend to be dramatically explosive. Rather, runny lava oozes out of a vent or series of vents. It eventually cools and hardens. After repeated flows, a gently sloping mountain is formed.

Molten rock meets the sea on Hawaii's south coast.

Driving along sections of the Big Island, you pass through black lava fields. Teenagers use white chunks of ocean coral to make letters against the black background and spell out messages to their friends. Nearer the volcano, lava heats the ground like an oven. Orange molten stripes shine among the black rocks. In places, lava pours into the churning ocean in red-hot waterfalls.

The volcanic activity on the Big Island is so intense that the early Polynesians believed Pele, their fire goddess, caused eruptions whenever she was angered by other gods or mortals. Like the lava that suddenly spouts out of cracks in the Earth, Pele was a changeable creature—sometimes she took the form of an old woman, sometimes a white dog, sometimes a beautiful maiden.

Novelist James D. Houston has described what it's like to walk over Hawaii's volcanic zones:

> Respect is too mild a word . . . [You begin] to see why old Hawaiians made all the lava places sacred, realms of wonder and glowing heat, gorgeous and fearsome. The spectacle surrounds you, and you want to give it a name, whatever comes rising from the treeless plain, and you see why the spirit that inhabits such a place [Pele] has been called possessive and wild and demanding and seductive in her beauty, impulsive and changeable. . . . The rock you step on can be four hours old or four hundred years old, or four thousand. The ancient and the new live side by side, the black rock and the seething red, the life of the surface and the life of the underworld, the fixed look of what has been here a while and the surging will of what is yet to become.[2]

Understanding this "surging will" was the goal of researchers working at Jaggar's HVO. Over the years, HVO scientists pioneered most of the monitoring methods still in use, like seismic and ground deformation analysis. Until 1980, however, HVO volcanologists wondered how much of the information they'd learned at the predictably oozing Kilauea would apply to a totally different type of beast, the explosive volcano.

When Mount St. Helens showed signs of awakening in 1980, HVO scientists realized they had their first chance to find out. "We were just a juvenile science [back then]," recalled Carolyn Driedger.[3]

That was about to change.

Mount St. Helens

Located in southwestern Washington State, Mount St. Helens's snowcapped peak is part of the Cascade Mountain range. At its base lies tranquil Spirit Lake. One woman who vacationed near Spirit Lake remembered, "Its 500 year old conifers [pine trees] shaded the lake and created a soft duff of twigs and needles underfoot. Winter nights were eerily quiet. On summer mornings, hardly a canoe disturbed the lake's still blue waters. On summer evenings, families lounged around fragrant campfires while the setting sun disappeared behind distant ridges. During these moments, perhaps a dog barked or a child shouted, but mostly there was the sound of lake water lapping its own slow lullaby."[4]

The peacefulness of this landscape was misleading. The Native Americans called Mount St. Helens *Louwala-Clough,* or "Smoking Mountain," after witnessing small steam explosions

Mount St. Helens in Washington State was a major tourist attraction for many years because of its beauty and seeming tranquility.

and pyroclastic flows pouring down its slopes. After 1857, how-ever, Mount St. Helens slumbered for more than a century. The YMCA set up a summer camp there. Logging companies worked the surrounding forests. Tourists came to enjoy the hiking and great fishing. The volcano's deadly potential was ignored by almost everyone, except for two volcanologists who were researching its eruptive past.

Dwight Crandall and Donal Mullineaux carefully surveyed the landscape and determined that past eruptions had created lahars that plugged valleys and dammed rivers. In 1975 they warned in *Science* magazine, "an eruption is likely within the next hundred years, possibly before the end of the century."[5]

On March 20, 1980, an earthquake at Mount St. Helens sent trees knocking against each other and a small avalanche crashing down the slopes past a group of snowmobilers. This earthquake was not like a normal earthquake. The seismograph was going crazy. In a regular earthquake, a seismograph draws a funnel shape that swings from side to side as the Earth moves and then comes slowly to rest when the earthquake stops. But Mount St. Helens was causing something entirely different. Instead of coming to rest, the seismograph kept recording movement. Based on the work done at HVO, the volcanologists knew that this type of seismic activity usually comes from rising magma. Over a period of days, they carefully watched the seismic readings and eventually determined that Mount St. Helens looked like it was getting ready to blow.

Tough Calls

At a briefing with local officials, Donal Mullineaux admitted that it was impossible to pinpoint exactly when such an eruption would occur. The problem, he explained, was that no one had enough experience with explosive volcanoes to know for certain.

One of the officials jumped up and demanded, "You mean to tell us that we as a nation can send a man to the moon and you can't predict if a volcano will erupt or not?"[6] We can't, Mullineaux acknowledged, pushing up his glasses and shaking his curly head, but that didn't mean there wasn't great danger.

The volcanologists distributed hazard maps showing which areas might be hit by avalanches, pyroclastic flows, and/or lahars. They wanted to make sure that the mountain and its surroundings were described as a hazardous Red Zone.

Few nonscientists heeded their warnings. Logging companies continued to work in the area, claiming to "know the mountain." Tourists hoping to see a volcano erupt flocked to the area and snuck around the blockades and past the harried park rangers. By the end of March, Mount St. Helens had become the state's number one tourist attraction. The *Tacoma News* reported, "People are swarming in from all over, putting their lives in danger. . . . Sunday, when the weather was clear, the road up to the mountain looked like downtown Seattle at rush hour."[7]

Earthquakes continued and enormous cracks opened up near the summit. A 450-foot (137-meter) bulge appeared on the north face due to magma pushing out the rock, deforming it. As the activity mounted, more scientists arrived to help carry out the variety of monitoring tasks. This was an unprecedented opportunity to gather information about a threatening volcano. Desperate to learn as much as they could, some scientists set up camps around Mount St. Helens that were dangerously close to the Red Zone.

"We were all struggling," recalled one of them, "Trying to figure out what to measure and how frequently do we measure it and what did it really mean? That was the problem. We were coming to an [explosive] . . . volcano shrouded in ice with the mental models of Hawaiian-style activity. How do you handle deformation here?"[8]

Suddenly, on May 18, the whole bulging north face of the mountain tore free. A massive avalanche of rock, snow, and mud raced downhill. Pent-up magma and gas blew out of the side of the volcano with a force equal to five hundred of the atomic bombs dropped on Hiroshima during World War II.

On a ridge 5.7 miles (9 kilometers) away from the volcano, David Johnston, a young volcanologist, radioed to the seismograph lab in Vancouver, Washington. "Vancouver! Vancouver! This is it!" he screamed. "Vancouver! Vancouver! Is the transmitter still working?"[9] Then he got hit by a pyroclastic flow.

These pyroclastic flows melted the snowcap, and lahars began rolling down the mountain. They were a hot-and-cold mixture of melting glacial ice and snow and burning-hot ash. A nineteen-year-old, Roald Reitan, who was camped on a riverbank 30 miles (48 kilometers) away, realized that something was very wrong. The crystal-clear river was turning milky and the blue sky had gone white. "Then I started seeing small sticks, then branches, then [tree] limbs floating by," he recalled. "We should get out of here," he shouted to his friend who was still asleep in the tent.[10] By the time they threw their tent in the car, the river was a muddy torrent. Looking upstream, Roald saw a wave of mud and "a railroad bridge that had broken off and was coming down the river sideways."[11]

Roald and his friend were swept 3 miles (4.8 kilometers) downstream in a terrifying flume of mud, ash, and crashing pine trees. When the mud fanned out in a wide plain, they were able to pull themselves to safety and eventually a National Guard helicopter pilot rescued them. "It was like flying in a milk bottle," another pilot recalled. "The sky and ground were the same color [from all the ash]."[12]

Throughout the nine hours of vigorous eruption, 500 million tons of ash fell. To understand how much that is, imagine a football field piled about 150 miles (241 kilometers) high with fluffy ash! Many people in the surrounding areas had to scoop ash out of their mouths in order to breathe, and one suffocated to

Mount St. Helens explodes as magma and gas blow out of the side of the volcano.

When Mount St. Helens erupted, 230 square miles (596 sq km) of trees were blown down—enough timber to build 150,000 homes. Two USGS scientists stand in the bottom right of the photo showing the enormous scale of the destruction.

death as his windpipe clogged. Thousands of deer, bear, and various small animals perished. Despite the volcano's fury, only fifty-seven people lost their lives, including a number of folks who ventured into the Red Zone.

The next day, Mount St. Helens was a gray moonscape of ash and steam. No birds sang; no squirrels chattered. Rescue helicopters circled the devastation, searching for any survivors. Ash continued to spurt out of the volcano, and when rain moved in, gray ashy mud fell from the sky.

Over the following weeks tons of ash were washed into the sewer systems as people cleaned off their streets and roofs. Dump trucks carted loads of ash to local landfills. Souvenir "ash" trays made of volcanic ash appeared in gift shops.

Experience Is Crucial

Directly after Mount St. Helens, funding for volcano-monitoring research increased tenfold, and the U.S. Geological Survey (USGS) created a permanent observatory called the Cascades Volcano Observatory (CVO). Here, volcanologists developed a suite of portable monitoring instruments that could be quickly deployed to any awakening volcano in the Cascade Mountain range, including Mount St. Helens. The Cascade Range stretches from northern California to British Columbia, Canada, and is dotted with volcanoes. All are of the same explosive type as Mount St. Helens. The cities of Portland and Seattle-Tacoma lie in valleys below Cascade volcanoes. A decade later the USGS set up another volcano observatory in Alaska, to monitor one hundred active volcanoes in that state.

By the end of 1986, Mount St. Helens had exploded with minor eruptions fifteen times, and the CVO volcanologists correctly predicted each one of them to within several hours. Despite these successes, they still weren't sure if the lessons they'd learned at Mount St. Helens would apply to other volcanoes. "Experience is crucial," one of them wrote. "We must be able to observe repeated episodes if we are to acquire knowledge of causes and to gain confidence in our predictions."[13]

After the eruption of the Nevado del Ruiz volcano in Colombia, South America, which triggered massive lahars killing 23,000 people, the USGS helped form the quick-response force that became known as VDAP (Volcano Disaster Assistance Program). Using portable volcano monitoring equipment, the team rushes overseas whenever a country officially requests help with a restless volcano.

VDAP's work saved many lives at Mount Pinatubo, and since that time, it has responded to crises in Central and South America, the Caribbean, Africa, Asia, and the South Pacific. In 1994, VDAP went to Papua, New Guinea, when the Rabaul volcano showed signs of erupting. VDAP distributed hazard maps and placed chalkboards around town to give up-to-the-minute volcano bulletins. They constructed models to simulate eruptions and showed films of the damage volcanoes can cause. Before the Rabaul volcano erupted on September 19, "fifty thousand people got up and walked out of town, even though they weren't told to do so by the official government scientists,"[14] said volcanologist Stanley Williams, who was on the scene. "The death toll could have been many thousands, because about 75 percent of the houses collapsed. It's a wonderful example of how people can be educated to save themselves."[15]

Today, more than twenty years after Mount St. Helens erupted, the forest is filling in and the wildlife is returning. But for the people who witnessed the eruption, nothing will ever be the same. One woman said, "When I bike through the blast zone now, I look at the [rocks] under my boots and remember that each of these little rocks has a violent story. Each one began underground as magma, surged up several miles to explode out of the volcano, cooled in midair, then pummeled the ground where I now walk. . . . Knowing this, I walk the land different than when I was a child. Back then, I fancied myself the mobile animal and the land an immobile backdrop."[16]

The USGS began monitoring Mount St. Helens in order to predict eruptions. Here, scientists measure the distance across a crack on the crater floor. A widening crack indicates that magma is rising and deforming the area, which could lead to an eruption. This work is especially dangerous because of the high temperature in the crack.

Dante II was built to investigate live volcanoes so that volcanologists could obtain information without being put in danger.

CHAPTER FOUR

Looking to the Future

In 1995 a new kind of volcanologist clambered into Alaska's Mount Spurr volcano. It was Dante II, a 10-foot-tall (3-meter) spiderlike robot similar to robots NASA uses to explore the Moon. Dante II was programmed to do various monitoring tasks and designed to remain in a crater for days. Its developer said that unlike a human scientist, "You can send it down and you don't have to worry about its safety."[1]

On the other hand, Dante II's price tag of $1.7 million meant that the robot wasn't exactly expendable, either. Further, it had some mechanical problems. Dante II made only one mission before malfunctioning. While robots might never replace human volcanologists, a more reliable one may be invented in the future that would be able to go places no human would dare venture.

The famous naturalist Louis Aggasiz once asserted that "the time for great discoveries is past. No student of nature should go out now expecting to find a new world." But, in fact, volcanoes offer some of the last uncharted terrain on our planet. In the past quarter century, our knowledge of this terrain has grown dramatically, and yet wish lists for the future are long because there is still so much to learn. Driving this quest is the volcanologists' awareness that people can die if volcanic events either don't happen as expected or happen much bigger than they predicted. Hoping to make more accurate hazard assessments in the future, many volcanologists have been heading into the lab.

One of these scientists, Richard Iverson, has built a 310-foot-long (95-meter) sloping trough. He dumps 40 tons of mud behind a steel dam at the top and then yanks that dam open. The mud roars down the steep flume and slogs out onto a flat stretch of ground below. Iverson takes measurements about the speed and behavior of the mud. He then makes computer models based on this data, which he hopes will help volcanologists better predict the path of real-life lahars.

Volcanologists agree that a big goal for the future is to put more volcanoes under the microscope. In the 1990s scientists were keeping an eye on roughly 150 active volcanoes, while "we should be monitoring a thousand," said one volcanologist.[2] As of today there aren't enough volcanologists or enough funds to monitor all these restless volcanoes. This means that sometimes difficult decisions have to be made about which ones to focus on.

Tragedy in Goma

In January 2002, Mount Nyiragongo in Africa erupted and poured lava into the town of Goma (population 500,000). For fifteen years an unpaid local volcanologist named Dieudonne Wafulah had been studying the volcano. With only a couple of battered seismometers, he managed to detect many pre-eruption warning signs. Wafulah tried to get funding to do more research, but he was turned down because Nyiragongo is the kind of volcano that oozes lava rather than explodes. "Although the lava moves quite fast going down the flanks [with this type of volcano], once on flat land it moves quite slowly so people can get out of the way," explained Brian Baptie, a volcanologist at the British Geological Survey.[3] Wafulah was told there were other more dangerous volcanoes that needed monitoring instead.

A week before the eruption, Wafulah sent urgent e-mails to everyone he could think of, saying that the volcano was heating up. The United Nations and the French Group for the Study of Active Volcanoes finally agreed to fund a survey team. Before they could arrive in the Congo, however, the volcano erupted and 40 percent of Goma was covered in molten rock, leaving 10,000 families homeless.

As volcanologist Thor Thordarson put it, for people in the field of volcanology there is "a continuous challenge to acquire more knowledge and do better. In their own way volcanoes remind us that despite our enormous achievements in the field of science and technology, we have still a long way to go before attaining a comprehensive understanding of what makes Mother Earth tick."[4]

USGS scientists take college students on a hike up to the crater of Mount St. Helens.

CHAPTER FIVE

Become a Volcanologist!

"The best part [of being a volcanologist] is being able to work outside in beautiful wild places with outstanding people," said scientist Tina Neal. "It is thrilling to make contributions, however small, to the accumulating understanding of volcanoes and volcanic process."[1]

If you're interested in becoming a volcanologist, the USGS recommends you prepare by taking as much math, chemistry, and physics as possible in high school. To date, very few colleges offer classes in volcanology, but the basic information you'll need is

TOUTLE RIVER

ST. HELENS LAVA DOME

ST. HELENS EAST

HOOD

Willie Scott, the scientist in charge of the USGS Cascades Volcano Observatory in Vancouver, Washington, studies a seismographic recording of an intense earthquake in 2001.

taught in geology programs. If you go to school in the American West, Hawaii, or Alaska, you'll probably get a chance to see volcanoes on geology field trips.

With a bachelor of science degree you can work as an assistant or technician mapping volcanoes or analyzing rock chemistry under someone else's direction. However, if you want to be a full-fledged volcanologist, you'll need an advanced degree such as a master's or doctorate.

A Variety of Volcanologists

Not all volcanologists work with threatening volcanoes. Many teach in universities and focus on specialized fields of research. For example, some concentrate on one particular volcanic product like steam or ash, others become experts at mapping lava flows, and some study the inner Earth. Volcanologist Steve Mattox said he worked on a project analyzing "the geochemistry of volcanic rocks in Utah. The field work was fun, but they were old dead volcanoes. The lab work was long (years) and at times tedious. But eventually I learned things about those volcanoes that no one knew before. That was exciting."[2]

Even the volcanologists who work on the edge with dangerously active volcanoes must balance their time in the field with hours spent at their desks. They carefully analyze data, write up results, develop theories, apply for grants, and publish papers.

Whatever their specialty, volcanologists tend to feel that they have some of the best jobs around, especially when they're out in the field and face-to-face with a real volcano. Volcanologist Kathy

Cashman fondly remembered her trip to Antarctica to study the Erebus volcano:

It was amazing. The volcano is 13,000 feet [3,962 meters] high and it was probably 20 or 30 below zero on the top. There is a great big crater in the top of the volcano with very, very steep sides. We would walk up to the top and lie down on our stomachs and look down. If you looked way down you could see the lava lake—red lava with a black crust, and the whole lake circulating. . . . You could feel the heat from it . . . It's very humbling. Antarctica is a particularly humbling environment altogether and to have a volcano in the middle of it is even more humbling! That's certainly part of what draws me to this field. It's good for us human beings to feel small.[3]

Glossary of Terms

ash: Fine dustlike particles formed during an eruption. Unlike the fluffy ash that comes from burning wood or paper, volcanic ash is hard and does not dissolve in water. It is extremely abrasive, like ground-up glass.

COSPEC: A device that measures volcanic gas; short for "*cor*relation *spec*trometer."

CVO: Abbreviation for Cascades Volcano Observatory.

fissure: A crack in the rock of a volcano from which lava often erupts.

fumarole: A vent from which volcanic gases escape into the atmosphere.

HVO: Abbreviation for Hawaiian Volcano Observatory.

lahars: Volcanic mudflows.

lava: Molten rock once it reaches the Earth's surface. Volcanologists also use the word *lava* to refer to the hardened deposits of flows.

magma: Molten or partially molten rock beneath the Earth's surface.

magma chamber: A reservoir of molten rock beneath a volcano.

pyroclastic flow: The ground-hugging avalanche of burning gas, ash, and rock fragments that can race down a volcano's slopes during an eruption.

seismometer: A device that measures ground vibrations, primarily from earthquakes.

tectonic plates: The dozen or so massive pieces that the Earth's surface is broken up into. Many volcanoes occur along their boundaries.

tephra: Pieces of rock and ash that blast into the air during an explosive volcanic eruption.

USGS: Abbreviation for Unites States Geological Survey.

VDAP: Abbreviation for Volcano Disaster Assistance Program.

volcano: A vent through the Earth's surface from which magma and gases erupt.

Source Notes

Introduction

1. Rose Willock, "The Sound of Thunder," *Essence,* January 1998, p. 89.
2. Chana Steifel, "Fighting the Volcano: A SWAT Team of Scientists Tackles the Ultimate Challenge," *Science World,* November 17, 1997, p. 18.
3. Stanley Williams and Fen Montaigne, *Surviving Galeras* (Boston: Houghton Mifflin, 2001), p. 5.
4. Lisa Stiffler, "St. Helens Blew the Lid off Geology, Too." [Online] Available at http://seattlepi.nwsource.com/mountsthelens/ring 09.shtml, May 9, 2000.
5. Charles A. Wood, "Have You ever Seen A Volcano Erupt?" [Online] Available at http://volcano.und.nodak.edu/vwdocs/frequent_questions/grp10/question699.html, July 29, 2002.
6. Williams and Montaigne, p. 6.

Chapter One: Predicting Eruptions

1. Lisa Stiffler, "St. Helens Blew the Lid Off Geology, Too." [Online] Available at http://seattlepi.nwsource.com/mountsthelens/ring09. shtml, May 9, 2000.
2. Stanley Williams and Fen Montaigne, *Surviving Galeras* (Boston: Houghton Mifflin, 2001), p. 2.
3. Scott Rowland, "How Do Volcanologists Predict Volcanic Eruptions?" [Online] Available at http://volcano.und. nodak.edu/vwdocs/frequent_questions/top_101Studying?Studying2.html, January 7, 2002.
4. Ben P. Stein, "Eruption! A Survivor's Tale," *Science World,* February 10, 1995, p. 18.
5. Stein, p.19.
6. Williams and Montaigne, pp. 4–5.

7. Stein, p.19.

8. Peter Tyson, "Under the Volcano," *Technology Review,* January 1996, p. 45.

Chapter Two: Eruption! Volcanologists on the Edge

1. Dick Thompson, *Volcano Cowboys: The Rocky Evolution of a Dangerous Science* (New York: St. Martin's Press, 2000), p. 235.

2. Thompson, p. 269.

3. Thompson, p. 267.

4. Thompson, p. 278.

5. Thompson, p. 280.

6. Louis Arana-Barradas, "Out of the Ashes: After Mount Pinatubo Nearly Buried It, Clark Air Base Bounced Back." [Online] Available at http://www.findarticles.com/cf_0/m01BP/11_45/80932425/p1/article.Jhtml?term=Arana-Barradas, November 2001.

7. "Starting Over a Decade After Pinatubo's Eruption." [Online] Available at http://www.findarticles.com/cf_0/m0WDP/2001_June_18/75831340/p1/article.jhtml?term=Bacolor, June 18, 2001.

Chapter Three: History of Volcano Monitoring

1. Haraldur Sigurdsson, *Melting the Earth: The History of Ideas on Volcanic Eruptions* (Oxford: Oxford University Press, 1999), p. 63.

2. James D. Houston, *The Last Paradise* (Norman: University of Oklahoma Press, 1998), p. 323.

3. Lisa Stiffler, "St. Helens Blew the Lid Off Geology, Too." [Online] Available at http://seattlepi.nwsource.com/mountsthelens/ring09.shtml, May 9, 2000.

4. Christine Cotasurdo, "Remembering Spirit Lake." [Online] Available at http://www.fs.fed.us./gpnf/mshnvm/new_chapters/new.html, January 31, 2002, p. 1.

5. Ed Klimasauskas, "Mount St. Helens Precursory Activity." [Online] Available at http://vulcan.wr.usgs.gov/Volcanoes/MSH/May18/MSHThisWeek/intro.htm, March 5, 2001.

6. Dick Thompson, *Volcano Cowboys: The Rocky Evolution of a Dangerous Science* (New York: St. Martin's Press, 2000), p. 34.

7. Thompson, p. 46.
8. Thompson, p. 82.
9. Mike Barber, "In Seconds, A Mountain and Many Lives were Lost." [Online] Available at http://seattlepi.nwsource.com/mountsthelens/erup08.shtml, May 8, 2000.
10. Barber, p. 1.
11. Neil Modie, "Memories of Awesome Power, Silent Fury." [Online] Available at http://seattlepi.nwsource.com/mountsthelens/surv15.shtml, May 15, 2000.
12. Barber, p. 6.
13. Thompson, p. 156.
14. Peter Tyson, "Under the Volcano," *Technology Review,* January 1996, p. 45.
15. Tyson, p. 45.
16. Cotasurdo, p. 1.

Chapter Four: Looking to the Future
1. Ben P. Stein, "Eruption! A Survivor's Tale," *Science World,* February 10, 1995, p. 18.
2. Peter Tyson, "Under the Volcano," *Technology Review,* January 1996, p. 45.
3. Chris Tomlinson, "Lava Flow Sets Fire to Congo City: 40 Reported Dead," *Boston Globe,* January 20, 2002, p. A3.
4. Tari Mattox, "Thor Thordarson." [Online] Available at http://volcano.und.nodak.edu/vwdocs/interview/Thor.html, December 6, 2001.

Chapter Five: Become a Volcanologist!
1. Tari Mattox, "Tina Neal." [Online] Available at http://volcano.und.nodak.edu/vwdocs/interview/Tina.html, December 6, 2001.
2. Steve Mattox, "Do You Have a Job Description for a Volcanologist?" [Online] Available at http://volcano.und.nodak. edu/vwdocs/frequent_questions/grp2/question311.html.
3. Tari Mattox, "Kathy Cashman." [Online] Available at http://volcano.und.nodak.edu/vwdocs/interview/Kathy.html, December 6, 2001.

Further Reading

Nonfiction

Bredeson, Carmen. *Mount St. Helens Volcano: Violent Eruption.* Berkeley Heights, NJ: Enslow Publishers, 2001.

Durieux, Jacques. *Volcanoes.* New York: Harry N. Abrams, 2001.

Haduch, Bill. *Volcano!: An Explosive Tour of Earth's Hot Spots.* New York: Dutton Books, 2001.

Lauber, Patricia. *Volcano: The Eruption and Healing of Mount St. Helens.* Glenview, IL: Scott Foresman, 1993.

Ritchie, David, and Alexander E. Gates. *The Encyclopedia of Earthquakes and Volcanoes.* New York: Facts On File, 2001.

Thompson, Dick. *Volcano Cowboys: The Rocky Evolution of a Dangerous Science.* New York: St. Martin's Press, 2000.

Thompson, Luke. *Volcanoes.* Danbury, CT: Scholastic Library Publishing, 2000.

Van Rose, Susanna, and James Stevenson. *Eyewitness: Volcano and Earthquake.* New York: DK Publishing, 2000.

Williams, Stanley, and Fen Montaigne. *Surviving Galeras.* Boston: Houghton Mifflin, 2001.

Fiction

Campbell, Eric. *The Shark Callers.* Orlando, FL: Harcourt, 1994.

Kehret, Peg, and Samuel Beckoff. *Volcano Disaster.* New York: Aladdin Paperbacks, 1998.

Mitchell, Nancy. *Raging Skies: Book Two: The Changing Earth Trilogy.* Fremont, CA: Lightstream Publications, 1999.

Web Sites

Cascades Volcano Observatory: vulcan.wr.usgs.gov/

Hawaiian Volcano Observatory: hvo.wr.usgs.gov/volcanowatch/
current_issue.html

Italy's Volcanoes: www.geo.mtu.edu/~boris/STROMBOLI.html

Make a Volcano Model: www.giseis.alaska.edu/Input/lahr/taurho/volcano/
volcano.html

NOAA Satellite Volcano Images: www.osei.noaa.gov/Events/Volcano/

NOVA Online Deadly Shadow of Vesuvius: www.pbs.org/wgbh/nova/vesuvius/

Smithsonian Global Volcanism Program: www.nmnh.si.edu/gvp/index.htm

Stromboli Volcano Online: www.educeth.ch/stromboli/index-e.html

U.S. Geological Survey Volcano Hazards Program: volcanoes.usgs.gov/

U.S. Volcano Disaster Assistance Program:
volcanoes.usgs.gov/About/Where/VDAP/main.html

Volcano Education: www.volcanolive.com/education.html

Volcanoes: Can We Predict Eruptions?: www.learner.org/exhibits/volcanoes/

Volcanoes Online: library.thinkquest.org/17457/english.html

Volcano Observatories: volcanoes.usgs.gov/About/Where/WhereWeWork.html

Volcano World: volcano.und.nodak.edu/vw.html

Index